Finding a Voice for the Love of Dogs

Sadie and Chudley: A Story of Healing after Tragedy

A. E. Palmer

The opinions expressed in this manuscript are solely the opinions of the author and do not represent the opinions or thoughts of the publisher. The author has represented and warranted full ownership and/or legal right to publish all the materials in this book.

Finding a Voice for the Love of Dogs
Sadie and Chudley: A Story of Healing after Tragedy
All Rights Reserved.
Copyright © 2016 A. E. Palmer
v2.0

Cover Photo © 2016 A. E. Palmer. All rights reserved - used with permission.

This book may not be reproduced, transmitted, or stored in whole or in part by any means, including graphic, electronic, or mechanical without the express written consent of the publisher except in the case of brief quotations embodied in critical articles and reviews.

Sadie and Chudley Inc.

ISBN: 978-0-578-18331-2

PRINTED IN THE UNITED STATES OF AMERICA

Dedication

This book is dedicated to all the dogs and the people who love and care for them. If you have ever loved a dog, you know its spirit and soul is like no other. Their love and loyalty is remarkable, like no human's. They cannot speak, and yet they have the ability to teach us so much about how to live genuinely.

Table of Contents

Chapter 1 Thoughts 1
Chapter 2 Our Family 3
Chapter 3 Tragedy Strikes 7
Chapter 4 Healing 15
Chapter 5 Finding Love, Peace, and Strength through
    Amazing Souls of the Universe and Our Badass Friend 18
Chapter 6 Enormous Outpouring of Love 20
Chapter 7 Humbled to Our Core 34
Chapter 8 Finding a Voice and Rights for Animals 36
After Log: Thank yous, Mahalos, Gratitude, Love,
    and Appreciation to Many Souls 39
Photo Collection: Sadie and Chudley and Their Friends,
    including Dreyfus 41

CHAPTER 1
Thoughts

Every single person in this world has a story. We each have to face one, if not many, hardships and challenges in some form. That's the way life goes. Nobody gets out of this place alive, and the tidal waves will hit you. No one, unfortunately, is immune. It's a bumpy road, a continuous journey, and a lifelong learning experience. Life is a lot like surfing. Some days you get up and ride the sweetest waves, while other days you crash and burn. Some surfers follow common courtesy and ocean etiquette, while some, well, they have their own idea of how to approach each wave, and don't adhere or care about the surfer norms. It's how we ride the waves in life.

Life is crazy. *Humans can be some of the craziest.* If you're a dog lover or animal lover, you understand that they have that innate ability to *love no matter what*. They don't care what race, religion, or gender you are. They don't care how much money you have in the bank or what prestigious university you attended. They just love you *for you*. They live life in the moment. They are loyal, loving, simple companions, who, if humans would pay more attention, could teach us a lot about honesty, compassion, kindness, and respect. Perhaps the world would be a more loving and peaceful place. Since this is a story about dogs, what better way to begin than by sharing some of our favorite dog quotations?

"Until one has loved an animal, part of their soul remains unawakened."-Anatole France

"If there are no dogs in heaven, then when I die I want to go where they went."-Will Rogers

"To my mind, I hold that the more helpless a creature, the more entitled it is to protection by man from the cruelty of man.

The greatness of a nation and its moral progress can be judged by the way its animals are treated."-Mahatma Gandhi

CHAPTER 2
Our Family

Some background before I get started on our story.

We are big animal lovers. My husband, Andy, was an animal science major in college. He and our son, David, even take the time to pull over on the country road they take to their favorite golf course to help get a snake off to the side. We marvel at the praying mantises that appear in our yard each summer and the cottontail bunnies that nibble on the grass. We somehow have beautiful dragonflies gracing us with their beauty and presence. Almost every kind of bird visits and drinks from our birdbath. They are amazing to watch and listen to. Even the squirrels that use our fence like a superhighway entertain us. There's something about animals that ground us. They connect us with the earth and remind us of how to live life and *live simply*. Nature is a beautiful thing.

My first nine years of life were spent in the countryside of West Sussex, England. I grew up watching the classic TV show *All Creatures Great and Small*. I would sit in awe and dream of being part of the vet crew, running from farm to home, helping to save animals. I even imagined the green "Wellies" (Wellington boots) I would wear, and the car I would get around in was a vintage-green Land Rover. I would have dogs surrounding me while living in a picturesque country cottage.

The cottage would have a warm, welcoming, cozy hearth. The smell of manure still conjures up happy thoughts of being around animals on a farm.

Flash forward to where we are at this moment, and life turned out differently, as it usually does, but it's not too far from my early childhood dream. I live in a beautiful "cottage" home in California. Instead of Wellington boots, I wear flip-flops, and instead of a Land Rover, I drive a Honda Pilot. Our family is all about animals. From the National Geographic channel to *National Geographic* magazine to watching Cesar Millan, "The Dog Whisperer," we love nature and animals. Our fourteen-year-old son has volunteered with Pound Puppy Rescue and Canine Companions. He has a huge goldfish named Brodo that he won at last year's church carnival. He has an African frog called DJ Man that he received from one of his grandmas when he was in first or second grade.

We used to have two beautiful Labrador retrievers. Now we only have the spirit of our two beloved dogs, Sadie and Chudley, who recently passed. Before they existed, we had a Lab rescue named Chablis. Before her, we had a Lab named Maggie and a Golden retriever named Chelsea. Before them, I grew up with a Lab rescue named Sunny. We *would have* cats, but unfortunately, I am allergic to their fur. I love cats. My son and hubby love to remind me, giving me the stink eye, that I am the reason we have no cats. Sigh.

We live in a neighborhood and a community that loves their dogs. They love their cats. They love their pets. And for the most part, they love animals. It's a welcoming, dog-friendly town. People are out every day with their four-legged friends, and it really evokes a nice sense of community, connection, and camaraderie. Dogs bring people together. Folks you don't know will automatically strike up a conversation with you about your dog, or by telling you about their dog. It's a great way to bond and make new friendships. Because our community is only a short trip from the coast, you see plenty of dogs with their families enjoying the marvel of the beach. It's pure paradise.

We got Miss Sadie, our sweet yellow Lab, when our son was in kindergarten. We thought that these two would grow up together, and as David is our only child, Sadie would be a four-legged sibling to him, and a four-legged child to us.

Sadie was referred to as a "red fox Labrador retriever" and had the energy of an Energizer bunny. She was the cutest puppy. Sadie made people stop when we were out, as she was the typical American Lab poster doggy. She melded into our family right away. She was our beloved companion-loyal, loving, fun, and full of kisses. She protected our home from two different attempted burglaries. Sadie was the first dog we knew who actually buried her bones in the backyard. Quite a feat.

When our son was in the fourth grade and Sadie was four, I thought a furry friend and sibling for Sadie would be a great fit for our family. Three humans, two doggies, one big happy family. Our good friends and neighbors down the road already had two chocolate Labs, Jasmine and Angus. Their chocolaty-brown coats always made me think of the teddy bears I'd had growing up. There was something unique and special about their fur that I found endearing.

I looked in the local paper and found a chocolate Lab litter nearby that had only one pup left, a male. I had never had a male dog. My husband had male Weimaraners growing up, so he was familiar with the whole "male" way of dog life.

We drove up to the site. It was way out in the mountains-Boonville, if you will. I was slightly nervous that we'd never make it out alive. Cell service was zilch, and this place looked more like a camp than a home. But to each his own, right? Brave faces on, we waited and then met the lady who owned the land. They had pigs, the ones you have for bacon; goats; horses; all kind of animals. She brought out this furry, scruffy, lovely pup. Andy was the first to hold him.

To quote Andy, "He immediately snuggled into my chest. He was a snuggle bear." If you knew our family, you'd know this was something I had always longed for: a snuggler. My two men and Sadie were not snugglers. I, on the other hand, *loved* to snuggle and cuddle. It took seconds for our family to fall in love with this little guy. His fur was ragged, and he was quite desperate for love, care, a family, and a home. I recently had discovered a British animated greeting card company called Jacquie Lawson. There, in one of Lawson's beautiful cards, was a chocolate Lab named Chudleigh. I adored the name. We would name our newfound family member, Chudley. Upon hearing that name, the lady laughed, and said, "Well, okay then!" Off we drove with our new baby bear, David holding him on the short drive home in the backseat. He snuggled the whole way.

When we got home, Sadie greeted us and sniffed this new, tiny ball of fur. This chubby pup thought Sadie was God. He was very happy to find another four-legged friend, and the two of them checked each other out. Sadie was gentle, kind, and as welcoming as we could have wished for. This was going to be a great fit to complete our family. By the evening, she was gently playing tug-of-war with Chudley in the softest way possible. We captured it on video. It melts our hearts every time we watch it.

Sadie basically helped raise and train sweet Chudley. He was the most easygoing pup we had ever had. He wanted to chill and be with his humans, his pack, as much as possible. Snuggling was his goal. We were a-okay with that! We think that because he only saw his older sister peeing by squatting, he never learned or thought to raise his leg like most male dogs do. He was a goofy, sweet-natured, gentle guy, with a heart full of love. Chudley wanted nothing more than to please. Both of them were that way. They never bolted, and whenever we came home, even if we were only gone for five minutes, they greeted us like royalty with oodles of love as if we had been gone for an eternity. No human does that. That's another beautiful trait of a loved dog.

CHAPTER 3
Tragedy Strikes

We were going about our normal routine one warm spring morning. Life was pretty status quo. We were a happy family of five, but you have to remember, two of our family members were our beloved dogs. We've always been a family with dogs. *Dogs make us better people.* Dogs teach us how to live life authentically and to love unconditionally.

Our son's eighth grade school year was coming to a close, and summer was on the horizon. Memorial Day weekend was beckoning us. California has some of the best weather, and that morning, there were blue skies, sparkling sunshine, and birds singing their spring medleys. It was a true California beauty of a day.

Sadie, Chudley, and I scampered out the front door for our usual morning walk. We always carried an armada of doggy poop bags, as with two, you had to be doubly armed. Our walks were more like therapy. Being outside in the fresh air, moving, talking with your best friends, and knowing how much your dogs loved these walks too was *as fulfilling as it gets*. We would meet up with our friend and neighbor, Tacey, and her Great Pyrenees rescue dog, Dreyfus. Our route consisted of winding through our charming neighborhood. Chudley worshipped Dreyfus. Every time he saw him, he would jump up and kiss him on his snout as if to say, "Hey, big buddy! I'm so excited! I love you! Let's walk our 'hood." Dreyfus, who is as stoic and majestic as they come, would smile and give Chudley that look like "You're okay, buddy. You're oh-kay. I like you too." Sadie, on the other hand, was more serious about getting on with the actual walk, although she would share some kisses with Dreyfus as well, and with Chudley, her younger, goofy, lovable brother, whom she helped raise.

We had all just met on the side of the road and greeted each other. The town where we live does not have sidewalks. When you're out for a walk or a bike ride, you quickly learn to stay as close to the side of the road as you can. Too many people drive like bats out of hell on residential streets. Our neighborhood had tried putting up signs that read "Drive Like Your Kids Live Here," but some people complained they were an eyesore, and one night they all vanished, never to be found or seen again. Life, the world, and people sure can be bizarre.

My eyes were looking at Tacey's face, and we were just about to turn and start walking our route. I remember hearing the faint sound of a diesel truck coming down the street from behind me. The next thing I knew, a massive truck had somehow barreled into us. Sadie and Chudley were being tossed, mangled, and tumbled underneath. I lay on the ground and had an instant feeling that this might be my last day and to prepare for it to hurt *a lot*. The shock, horror, and adrenaline were all racing at lightning speed in my head, my heart was breaking, and *my soul was crushed*.

Seconds later I got up and saw Sadie and Chudley on the side of the road. Horrified, terrified, and sickened, I knew there would be little or no hope for their survival, a memory that haunts me. *A permanent scar on my heart.* Luckily, Tacey and Dreyfus were physically unscathed, and Tacey quickly dialed 911 as we watched the large truck drive off down the road. Screaming, shaking, and in panic mode, I desperately tried to call my husband but kept getting no answer. A man came out from one of the nearby homes and asked if there had been a bad car accident. Were we okay? He had been in his back garden watering his plants and heard a loud crash that made him think two cars had collided. Within minutes, the paramedics, a fire truck, and the police arrived.

God must have been watching, as our sweet neighbor and friend, Lisa, was driving by on her way home from school drop-off. She saw the fire truck, ambulance, police, Sadie, Chudley, and me, all on the side of the road. She pulled over, got out of her Yukon, and offered to transport our babies to our vet for emergency medical treatment. I learned that day there is no emergency transport for injured pets. Thank God, Lisa had come to our aid. We frequently refer to her as a brave angel, as her timing could not have been better. Her courage to stop and offer help is one not everyone has. Tacey ran back to my house with Dreyfus to alert Andy, who was getting ready for work. Together, they ran as fast as they could to the terrible scene.

Everyone was in shock that such an event could happen and play out the way it did. My heart was beating so fast that I was having what the paramedics kept calling PVCs (premature ventricular contractions). The paramedics gently wheeled me off to our local hospital. Inside the ambulance, I got to know two incredibly kind souls, J and K. During that short ride, they told me about their experiences and love for their dogs from the past to the present. Good people carried me while the storm around me unfolded.

As I was wheeled into the ER, I realized that my life and my family's lives would never be the same. Tragedy had struck, and only in our worst nightmare would something like this happen. It was all surreal, a blur. If I had been an inch farther out on the road, my condition could have been a completely different story. I was a little tattered and torn on the outside, but on the inside I was falling apart. Everyone kept telling me that I was very, very *lucky*. I understood that. I was lucky to be alive and not maimed in any serious way. Internally though, *I felt broken*. I witnessed our two fur babies, our dogs, destroyed in a most violent and painful way. We were supposed to be doing our favorite activity, taking a walk. They were supposed to come home with me. This was our neighborhood. The sights and sounds kept playing over and over in my head. Had Sadie and Chudley saved my life? Quite possibly yes. Was I heartbroken? Most definitely yes.

While my physical wounds were being tended to, I could hear Andy on the phone with one of the vets. By the sound of his voice, I could tell it was not good news. Our Sadie had been severely injured. Andy lost it. This nightmare was real and it was happening. On the other hand, they couldn't quite tell yet if Chudley was as badly injured. Their goal was to stabilize him and transport him to a higher-care facility for more treatment and around-the-clock care.

I was released from the ER after I took an anxiety pill and wandered into the waiting room, where I was met by Tacey; her husband, Justin, who had left work to be by her side; our friend Erica, whom we call our "badass" friend (you will see why later on); and our friend Helen. All of us had that look of disbelief on our faces, that feeling and hope that we would all wake up from this horrible dream. Helen drove Andy, Erica, and me to the vet to see Sadie and Chudley. We walked into the back room, where Sadie was lying down, bandaged up and on major painkillers. We knew within minutes that we would have to make the decision to put her down. Her hindquarters had been completely crushed and broken as the truck rolled over her. It was brutal. We went over to see Chudley, who was surrounded by loving vet techs and thought there might be a chance that he would make it. Maybe there would be a little light in all of this darkness and chaos.

With tears and great sadness, we knew the most humane thing to do would be to let Sadie pass peacefully. We comforted and talked lovingly to her as her eyes gently closed and she took her last breath. This was excruciating for us. Losing one of our beloved dogs so suddenly after such a horrific incident was unreal. Our time at the vet felt surreal, just like everything else, as if this was happening in slow motion, yet it was all in real time, too fast for us to process. We left feeling numb, empty, dead, and paralyzed. Life had become a spinning blur of madness.

Upon returning home, we sat and wondered where this would all go, how we would get through this nightmare, and how we would break it to our fourteen-year-old son, who was, thankfully, at school going about his day. It felt as if we were floating uncontrollably in a land of fear, chaos, and loss.

As the afternoon came around, hundreds of people reached out to us in concern, offering their condolences. The love and support from everyone was humbling to our core. I wanted to keep walking, keep living, as difficult and different as it would be. Walking with our dogs was our happy family activity and an extremely therapeutic activity for me. I did not want to succumb to this new unwanted fear. I had a new fear of trucks. The sight and sound of them rattled my bones with panic. Sirens made me nervous. Walking on our neighborhood streets, or driving on any street, brought great anxiety to my veins and mind. I was feeling the aftereffects and doing my best to confront them and sit with them, while I prayed for healing. That evening, while there was still plenty of light outside, Andy and I walked down to the spot where this all happened. There we saw Sadie and Chudley's fur mashed into the asphalt. Our hearts sank into unspeakable levels of misery and shock. We also found the poop bag I was carrying that morning. We picked it up and carried it home with us. Ironically, it wound up being our last memento from Chudley Bear. Everything seemed illusory, and our hearts were shattered. This was happening, and it had happened.

The next day, our son went to school, as he had an eighth grade graduation project that had to be done in order to participate in the graduation ceremony. I served as a volunteer on the exhibition panel, while Andy stayed home and worked on insurance issues, making numerous phone calls to get help on how to handle all of this craziness. Andy visited Chudley at the critical care hospital and sent an update to me that he was somewhat stabilized. We all still carried some hope that he would pull through. After school that afternoon, we went as a family, including my mom (their grandma, who often looked after them), to pay Chudley a visit. We patiently waited until we could go into the room. There, we saw our baby hooked up to numerous tubes, including one for blood transfusions, which I had no idea animals could do. Vaguely listening to the vet explain Chudley's condition, we broke down into that deep, dark abyss filled with heavy sadness and shock. Andy was probably trying the hardest to listen and understand what the vet was communicating to us. It was again surreal and brutal.

In tears, we decided we needed a moment in a quiet room to discuss our thoughts on the state of our beloved Chudley. While we attempted to talk, in between heaving and sobbing wildly, my mom sat with Chudley, gently stroking his head and talking to him, telling him what a great dog and family member he was. She told him how much we all loved him and Sadie, and how sorry and heartbroken we were that this had happened. After some time, we agreed that as gut-wrenching as it would be, the most humane thing to do for Chudley would be to let him pass. While his bones weren't crushed, almost all of his vital organs were struggling to keep working. He wasn't able to use one of his front legs. Nerves had been damaged from tumbling under the truck. He was so broken, much more broken than we had realized the day before. It was the most brutal thing all over again. Two dogs in two days. A once happy family of five had been blindsided and demolished in a matter of seconds. We were now just three. We sat with Chudley and reiterated how much we loved him, how truly sorry we were, and how much we would miss him. He was a great dog. Sadie was a great dog. A part of us died that afternoon. Our dogs were better than human beings.

Dogs love you for who you are. They don't care how much money you have, what you look like, or where you live, they just want to live and love in the moment and be there with you, wherever you go. Animals are gifts from God, blessings with fur, who cannot speak yet teach us profound lessons in living authentically.

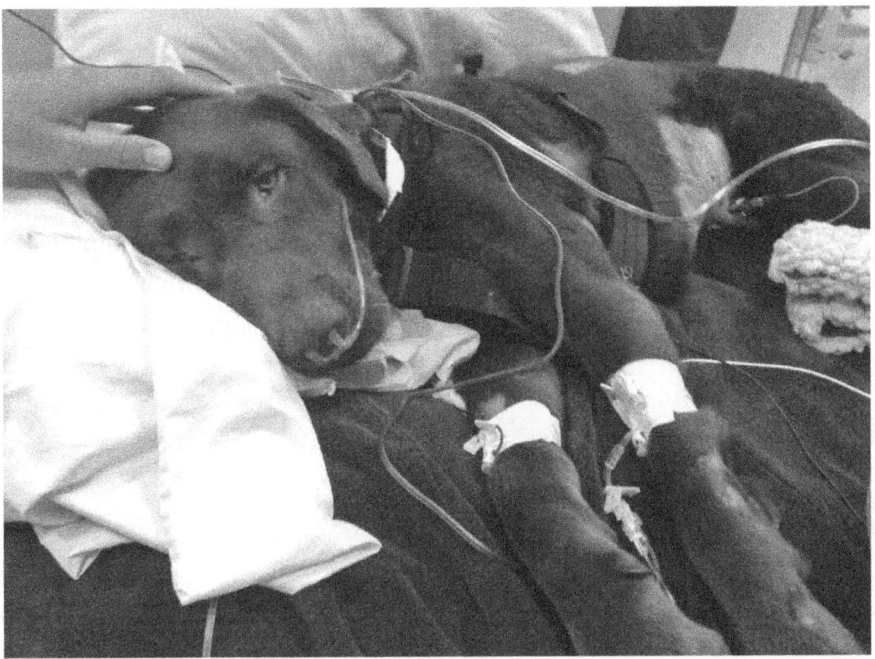

The next day, we all holed up in our home to mourn. I had to put a note on our front door, as the number of people coming to speak with us was overwhelming. We needed space and time together to let all of our pain and emotions out and to *grieve*. It was a complete sea of darkness.

This was an extremely difficult time for our family, as we very much wanted to seal away the pain and suffering, the tragic loss of our beloved dogs. We wanted to have some peace from this awful experience and start some kind of healing. For us, it's about healing our hearts and family, getting through this pain, and trying to gather some sort of strength, wisdom, understanding, and life lessons from this. Anytime someone loses a beloved pet, it is beyond hard. Your heart sinks and travels into depths of emptiness you never fathomed possible. Dogs love us like no human can. Sharing Sadie and Chudley's story is sharing their love and trying to bring some sort of light into all of this gloom. It is an attempt to bring a voice to animals and advocate for their rights and protection. Dogs do so much for us, and sadly, they do not receive the proper respect and care in the eyes of the world. **Animals make us better people.**

One way their story has already helped is at the hospital where Chudley was taken, the staff is using his story to help train some of their critical-care vet techs and doctors. They hope to help them remember that even amid all of the chaos that can happen, these animals are more than just pets. They are people's beloved family members.

CHAPTER 4
Healing

Somehow the universe had already helped me *before* this tragedy. I had been seeing a psychologist weekly for anxiety and depression. I learned at my next appointment that my doctor was also an animal advocate and a former Humane Society volunteer, and she had run a pet loss support group in the past. It was a most fortunate stroke of serendipity; my doctor couldn't have been a more perfect remedy to help mend my broken spirit.

Through our meetings I learned just how much our dogs were truly therapeutic for my health and well-being, mentally *and* physically. Our family was deeply mourning the tragic loss of our two most loving, kind, and happy members. I was living in a dark, peril-filled mind and body, feeling lifeless inside. I was heartbroken, full of wild anxiety. The memory of experiencing it all killed my spirit and soul. I had survivor's guilt up and down and all over me. I was mentally and emotionally enervated. My soul was permanently damaged. How could anything positive ever come out of this?

We live in a small home, graced with a beautiful front and backyard. Because our dogs were such a big part of our family, there were signs of them wherever we turned. They went everywhere with us. Neighborhoods, towns, roads, beaches, restaurants, coffee shops…

they were there with us. We didn't have the strength or will to put away any of their belongings. Our dogs were never backyard dogs. They were part of our lives, every day, every night. Some people might say, "Oh, get over it. They're just dogs." To us, they were our family. Every day letters, cards, and artwork of our dogs poured in from people we knew and people we had never met. Flowers, edible arrangements, and e-mails from tons of people reached us. It was beyond humbling.

We decided that to be true to ourselves, we would really try to keep on being a peaceful, loving family. Anger and vengeance would not work for us. There is too much anger and hatred already in our world. In order to heal properly, we needed to find the strength through all the pain; accept the circumstances, as much as we did not want to; and let go.

The sadness hits us in waves, ups and downs that strike unexpectedly. Our hope is to ride the waves; be there for each other; talk, listen, and support each other; and honor what we had and what we have now. Our aim to move forward, one day at a time, has been easier said than done but is a must for healing. I feel like I lost two of our family members. I feel broken and devastated over this. I feel like the worst human being in the entire world. On the polar opposite side, I feel lucky and fortunate, blessed to have had the times with Sadie and Chudley. Now I feel gutted. One of my favorite quotes is from Dr. Martin Luther King Jr.: "Forgiveness is not an occasional act, it is a constant attitude." This I really have to honor and practice.

Now that summer is here, we are finally coming up for air. It's still surreal and strange, and we struggle with the day-to-day absence of our Sadie and Chudley. Their absence is amplified by the ghostly quietness of the house. Our walks are oddly lonesome, and when our neighbors see us, they all know we are *that family* who tragically lost our two beloved dogs. To quote our son, "It's like life is dark and empty, and the dogs added so much color and joy." We got Chudley's ashes back the other day and are awaiting Sadie's. I found a beautiful statue of

St. Francis of Assisi (patron saint of animals) for our backyard, and we plan to scatter Sadie's and Chudley's ashes around that area. They loved their backyard.

We walk as a family during the California summer nights, as the sun is still up at 8:00 p.m. We walk the loop we used to do with our dogs. The heavy hearts are still there. We share numerous and entertaining memories of our times with our dogs and know we will never forget them. Writing has been one of my biggest sources of finding comfort.

I shake a lot, my heart pounds and races unexpectedly at times, and my worries become center stage when I think about what happened and where we are now. When I think about walking a possible furry friend in the future, I feel nauseous and nervous. I have that "what if…" anxiety running through my mind. The whole "life can change in the blink of an eye" fear. I pray that God will bless our family someday with another furry family member. It was an honor to have Sadie and Chudley in our lives. I feel utterly awful about how I lost them. I feel stuck in a black hole with no way out at the moment. I look forward to my therapy sessions more than ever. I try to keep breathing deeply and exhaling all of the toxic thoughts and feelings racing through my head.

As I sit and talk and cry with my therapist, I hope that from this great loss, some sort of light may possibly come from Sadie and Chudley's story. Maybe the laws will change and dogs and animals will not be viewed as property. They will receive more justice and more respect. People who abuse animals should be punished and fined. **Dogs bring so much to us.** Mine were part of my daily soul food, my therapy. My lifelong dream, ever since I was that little girl in the countryside of West Sussex, has been to promote animal welfare. I want to thank all of the animal advocates, the veterinarians, the therapy dogs and trainers, the angelic volunteers who help comfort and care for homeless animals, and the kind souls who understand and care about all of God's creatures.

CHAPTER 5

Finding Love, Peace, and Strength through Amazing Souls of the Universe and Our Badass Friend

We are in rebuilding mode. Our son starts high school in the fall, a monumental time in his life and ours. We want to start living and enjoying life to the fullest again. We love our simple life. We will find it again I am sure. I have faith.

Speaking of faith, this is where you will learn why we call our friend Erica our "badass" friend. There's an inside joke - well, not inside anymore - but within our little village of friends, we have a saying, "People suck." Our good friend and fellow animal lover, who happens to be a vet too, came up with that one. She hopes to write a book someday about that. There's another one, "People suck. Dogs don't." While there's a lot of truth to those two statements, this horrific experience gave us a whole new perspective about humanity. Sometimes when tragedy or hardship strikes, people rise to unprecedented levels of humanity, kindness, and compassion. The support that arose from this terrible loss was unbelievable. It was truly out of a movie or a tall tale.

Our badass friend Erica, probably on the evening of the accident, came up with the brilliant idea to start an online fundraiser to help us cover our enormous vet bills, an immediate need. So many people reached out to her when they heard about the incident, wanting to know how they could help. Erica is a genius. Her quick-witted thinking during a time of chaos created this idea. Unbeknownst to us, it spread like wildfire across Facebook. Within four short days, she had managed to raise $9,500! Our vet bills for two days were that big. We are not made of money. We are pretty simple folks, and we knew these vet bills would knock us down pretty hard. Upon learning about this incredible donation from the community and beyond (many people we had never met), we were brought to our knees.

Yes, some people do suck. But there were hundreds of people out there who did not suck, do not suck, and truly care. It was mind-boggling. We were humbled to the deepest depths of our once empty souls. There were no words to express and convey our deepest gratitude and thanks to all of the kind and generous individuals. I spent the next couple of days writing thank-you notes. **It was, and still is, most heart-warming, touching, and moving.** Humans can be decent and kind. Andy, who never had much faith in humanity to begin with, was beginning to see people through a whole new lens with hope.

Erica dropped off the check at our home, less than a week after the incident. As she walked off, we stood there in awe. She is one fierce, loving, creative, skilled, gifted, amazing soul of the universe. We thank God every day for having such a beautiful and kind friend like her in our lives. Erica, along with our other friends and our community, helped to lift us up, and bridge that gap between bills that needed to be paid and the long journey ahead to bring closure to this chapter in our lives. Erica, in our humble opinion, is like Lisa. Another great angel disguised in human form.

CHAPTER 6

Enormous Outpouring of Love

I am going to share some of the responses we received from people we know and others we have never met. They are truly *humbling and amazing*.

(I have not included their names, for privacy reasons.)

You are so kind to send us a thank-you letter for our donation! I just had to reach out and help where I could, seeing this senseless tragedy unfold before me. You have always been so supportive of the ML staff, and, Annie, you were always so great to see at Marshall Lane and always on hand helping everyone...to lose your two dogs that way is beyond fathoming. I am SO glad you are okay, Annie, and I am hoping that in time, your scars-both inside and out-can heal from this terrible incident.

Pets are definitely one of the best things a family can ever have! They love us unconditionally, make us laugh, make us relax, let us appreciate life's simple pleasures, and always seem wise beyond their years when we look into their kind eyes. Chudley and Sadie did this, and even more, by spreading their joy and wisdom through your postings and blogs on Facebook and Instagram. We gained our everyday wisdom through their reminders to relax, take it easy, and bring joy to others. They will be sorely missed!

Wishing you healing thoughts, prayers, and the courage to carry on as Chudley and Sadie keep their heavenly vigil. You are thought of daily!

You are most welcome, and please don't put any more thought into placing me; we have never met. Your situation simply broke my heart. Animals as a whole are my passion. Animal companions are so much more than "pets"; they are family. I cannot fathom the depth of your heartache and feeling of helplessness. I hope you are able to get past the anger sooner than later, and can focus all of your energy on recovering from what I am certain seems to be a nightmare from which you cannot awaken.

The weight in my heart is lessened knowing I alleviated, in some small measure, some of your stress.

Wishing you all a future filled with happy memories of Sadie and Chudley. I had posted that you should check out the Rainbow Bridge Poem, and I stand by that. It is what I envision heaven to be. But there is also another poem or prayer out there called "A Dog's Last Wish." This will be hard to read, and I don't know how you feel about adopting other dogs in the future (it is quite likely too soon), but this is a very lovely sentiment. But do have a tissue handy:

A Dog's Last Wish

Before human beings die, they write their last will and testament
To leave their home and all they have to those they love.

I would do such, if I could write, to a poor and desperate, lonely stray,
I would give my happy home, my bowl, my cozy bed, my pillow, and my toys.
The so loved lap, the tender stroking hands, the lovely voice, the place I had in someone's heart.
The love that at last helped me find a peaceful end, held firmly in a sheltering embrace.

When I die, please don't say, "I will never have a pet again, the loss is far too much to stand."
Choose a lonely, unloved dog and give him MY place.
This is my inheritance. The love I leave behind is all I have to give.

From a dog's perspective, about not mourning them in such a way that prevents you from adopting other dogs.

Hoping your memories of your beloved Sadie and Chudley help to mend your broken hearts. Be well.

Please don't feel bad about not being able to place me! We've actually never met, so this isn't surprising.

I heard about what happened through some of your neighbors and friends whom I happen to be friends with on Facebook. I was so saddened to hear you had lost both of your beloved dogs, and that made me think of how I would react if I lost my own Lab, Momo. I also lost two of my cats to unfortunate circumstances last year, which still leaves me in a vulnerable place, and I wanted to contribute what I could to helping your family get through this truly difficult time. I know from experience it can be a very long healing process.

I wish you and your family the best in this process, and I am glad that I could contribute, even a small amount, to alleviating some of the stress on your family. You are all in my thoughts :)

Your note is beautiful, thank you. Larry and I didn't even need to think twice about donating.

There hasn't been a day that has gone by since the accident that I haven't thought about what happened to you and your dogs. Blake was in tears when I told him about it. Sometimes it's just so hard to understand why things happen. You are always a ray of sunshine for everyone. You always see the positive and truly have a beautiful spirit.

I can't believe both of your dogs were just swept out of your life so quickly. It's just unbelievable. But, thank God you are okay. I'm just so so very sorry this happened to your family.

Hugs to you all.

There was no need for thanks, Anne, that's what friends are for. We want you to feel better fast.

I cannot begin to tell you how sad I have been reading your posts since the tragedy happened. Every night I pray for you to bring peace into your heart and know that your babies are in a good place. We believe that you will feel the souls of your dear dogs when they are reborn again so that never dies. You will feel them and their love in your heart forever-they were your family!

I am here for you if you need to chill, have a cuppa or a Cadbury's chocolate! Please call. I would love to sit and natter with you. We are here for you, dear friend, and we love you! We want to bring that sunshine back in your life and to embrace all the good things we still have in our lives that we are truly blessed with.

If you need anything, please let us know! Big hugs to David and Andy too. God bless you and embrace you in his comforting presence.

Love and hugs…

Don't worry your mind is fine. We don't know each other. I live in San Jose. I heard of your story and needed to do something. I too am a dog lover and can't imagine your loss. I too have two dogs. It's hard enough when a pet passes from old age, but in your case it's even more difficult.

I wish you and your family well. The body will heal, but it will take a little longer for the mind.

Don't take too long before letting another furry friend into your life. I believe the love of another dog may help your healing.

Please take care.

Thanks for the nice comments about Lisa and family. We agree! They are always there for their real friends and never afraid to get involved. So sorry about Sadie and Chudley. I never met them personally, except noses through the fence. ;-), but Lisa said they were great pups. We are glad Lisa was able to help you.

Thank you for your thoughtful note. We have never met. I saw the story of what happened to you and just wanted to help in some way. I love dogs and my heart breaks for all that you are going through. I have had Labs all my life. I lost my last Lab (Jonesy) three years ago. I could fill a lake with all the tears that I have cried for him. Jonesy was my best friend and soul mate. I rescued him from an animal shelter when he was two, and I was blessed to have him for fourteen years. I am so sorry for …you and your family. I know that you will heal in time. Your furry angels will be with you always. My thoughts and prayers are with you and your family. With much love…

What a beautiful note. I certainly didn't expect to hear from anyone, as I can't even imagine what a terrible time you're all going through. The reason you don't recall me is we've never met. Your story just broke my heart into pieces, and I saw the GoFundMe page and gave a little toward your vet bills. As an animal lover and owner of three dogs myself, I just couldn't imagine losing my babies and then having to face the monstrous vet bills. So very grateful that you were not seriously injured in the accident, and I do pray that you will find some comfort in knowing that people all around this country are praying for you.

We are only connected by the fact your tragic story touched my heart. I saw your story on Facebook.

I have three dogs I walk every morning and night and to think my babies could be taken away from me like yours is terrifying. I hope that all the good wishes you have received will help. And all your new and old friends paying off your vet bill is a small thing people can do to help when we really don't know what else we can do.

I am so sorry for the loss of your beautiful dogs. I hope in time your hearts heal and you can welcome new babies into your life. Big hugs to you and your family. Take care.

You are so thoughtful to take the time and send this note. You are most welcome, and it's honestly the least we could do. We'd give just about anything to be able to hit the rewind button so that it never happened, to have spared you all from going through this. Love the picture of your fur babies. Such sweet souls.

We love you. We are here for you. Take care of you and remember to applaud the little things. Sometimes success is simply remembering to breathe.

Love…

I have been thinking about you and your family a lot over the last week. We were so sorry to hear this news; our hearts just went out to you guys, and we wanted to help you in some small way.

I know how much your dogs meant to you, Andy, and David. I loved seeing all your posts on them. I totally understand the pain you are feeling. We now have three dogs of our own, and they become instant members of your family. To lose them in the way you did is devastating!

Please know that you are in our thoughts.

Sending you all lots of hugs and love…

Like so many others, I am thinking of you guys daily. I'm a person who prefers to retreat when I need to heal, so I sometimes assume others are the same way. When you are ready to venture out with some gal pals again, just raise the flag, send a text, post a note, and we will be there to distract you. No one wants you to have to relive or talk about things that make you sad. So just know, the army will be at your side whenever you feel ready. Until then, you have our good thoughts and silent blessings.

When we heard about what happened to you, Sadie, and Chudley, it brought us to tears. Same for the kids; they heard through the RHMS and ML grapevine what happened and were so sad. You (and your family) are so special to our community, and we all feel for you and want to do whatever we can to show our support and love.

Like you said, time will help the healing process, slowly day by day.

Please let us know if you need anything at all. We are here for you.

You and your family have been weighing heavy on our hearts. What a devastating loss, Anne. We continue to keep all of you in our thoughts and prayers. Please take care. xo

I think of you all so often (we all do) and can't imagine how difficult this time is for you.

I'm not surprised at the outpouring of support. You are all very special, and we love you and just want to help in any way we can.

Just keep taking it day by day, and a new version of your life will gently unfold…bringing new joy and more love.

I just know it. :)

Much love to you and to your two sweet angels as well.

We didn't do anything you wouldn't have done. As fellow dog *adorers*, our heart breaks for you all. We are just so glad you are okay, Anne. Love…

We are here for you, Andy, and David. As much as we'd like to help with the healing process (and will when we can), we know that this is mostly out of our hands and must be done alone and with close family. On the other hand, these bills are something we actually can help with. Along with your other friends and neighbors, we want you to continue healing without the unnecessary burden of thinking about bills. See you soon.

Love…

Thank you for the kind e-mail, Anne. But, honestly, you don't even need to worry about thanking me. I feel privileged to be your friend and grateful I could be of some help in this time. We pray for you and your family every night.

You are in our hearts and thoughts. I know it is very difficult, but please know you are very loved! And SO THANKFUL you are healthy! Take care, my friend!

So very thankful to have you in our lives! My heart aches for you and your precious family. Please know how much we care and know that you are being thought about and prayed for every day! I'm here whenever you need me! Coffee, wine, the beach, whatever! I would love to do my best to put a smile on your face!

Lots and lots of love!I

Thinking of you every day, dear Anne, and wishing I could take your pain away. Your babies were so lucky to have you for their mom. Sending you much love and hugs to help you heal.

Knowing you are loved is a gift from heaven. Thank you for being you. Looking forward to spending some time with you when you are ready.

Love, hugs, and God's blessings to you and your family.

I know! Where did our little kids go? Fun to see who they are becoming though.

Enjoy today. Such a big accomplishment for David (and his parents!).

P.S. I like that phrase "stitch my heart back together"... and the rest of it too. Happy to be here whenever needed. I feel like I've been mourning myself-for those two beautiful creatures, for your family's grief, and for some sense of security lost in the neighborhood. It helps me (and I'm sure the scores of your friends and family) to feel that I can help in some small way.

No apology is needed-you don't know me, and I don't know you. I am just a dog lover and have two of my own. I read your story on a friend's Facebook page and wanted to make a donation. I'm terribly sorry for your loss. I know my two mean the world to me as I'm sure yours did to you. I hope you and your family can find some comfort in your memories of your beautiful dogs. God bless.

I know that the light goes out. The sparkle in the eyes goes out. The world continues to turn without you when your life has come to a stop. Nothing makes you happy; in fact I had a guilty feeling if I smiled or wanted to laugh. And it hurt so deeply. I thought I would never smile or laugh and be content again.

Little by little without being conscious of it, I got interested in life again; my friends were great and supportive. It took me a long, long time to heal. Everybody is different.

Do not despair. Be gentle with yourself. Everything will pass. When? I cannot tell you, but I know for sure it will pass.

I wish I could have a magic wand to make this dark cloud disappear.

Thinking of your possible future new puppy, what her personality will be like. She will be so cute, will force your mind to watch this new life and not rehash the past. It is toxic. Marching on one day at a time is a great accomplishment.

I love you so much. I want the best for you.

I am here for you. Ask if I can help in anyway and I will.

Love, Mom

We have been so disturbed, sad, and upset about what happened to you. Such a tragedy. We are dog lovers and lost our dog, Chloe (she was fifteen), a couple of years ago. The loss is significant, and it is a loss of a family member. Two in your case. Given the tragic circumstances that you experienced, it is unimaginable. We are so sorry. Donating to your vet bills was the very LEAST we could do. If there is anything else you need, please don't hesitate to ask.

We now have a new dog, Coco, and she has filled a new place in our hearts, although we still often remember and talk about Chloe.

Sadie and Chudley were beautiful dogs. I feel like I know them. They are truly angels now.

Know that we continue to think of you often.

You are so right about missing your dog(s) more than a person, even one of your parents, because your daily life and routines are so wrapped around each other. Every hour seems to present a new opportunity to notice a dog(s) is gone. The little reminders are more painful than the big ones sometimes. The seemingly insignificant, silent, quirky moments you and your two little loves shared still happen, but you are without them. Baby steps, Anne. This too shall pass, or at least the pain will be muted. Everything will be all right one day.

Even without this unspeakable loss, you went through your own violent trauma and fright being hurt. I hope the support you have to help you cope-with even only that part-is strong and loving.

I hope I am not too much up in your grill. :) I know how it feels to lose a dog you truly love, and my heart goes out to you.

Take care, and I will continue to send all the good vibes I have to send to you. :)

As a Living Tribute

Two trees will be planted in
Tahoe National Forest (CA) in honor of

Chudley and Sadie

Long may they stand, reaching ever upward,
To embrace the light and warmth of the sky above.

This gift made possible by

The Urban Pooch

CHAPTER 7
Humbled to Our Core

It was incredible. We had no words to express how truly touched we were by the outpouring of love, kindness, generosity, and support from so many around and beyond us. At night, we would look up to the stars and wonder if our Sadie and Chudley were shining angels in the sky. I do believe in a heaven, and I also like to believe that our beloved animals, our other family members, and our friends can all be together again in the afterlife.

I know I struggle with surviving and the loss of two of our dear family members. I know our dear friend Tacey is having a tough time with surviving too.

It's been a haunting story to have been a part of, one we would gladly decline. We now wear our heads on a swivel when walking. People have commented that maybe my dogs were on extra-long leashes. They were not. We were all on the side of the road where pedestrians should be. It was simply split seconds of tragedy. If I had turned seconds earlier, perhaps I would have seen this truck coming and could have swiftly moved out of its way. It pains me to think about that, and it will linger in my gut forever as much as I try to let it go. My candle's inner flame that used to shine so brightly has lost its ability to ignite or glow.

We dream of having a new furry, four-legged friend join our family soon, but we are also very cautious. Scared. Scarred. Life can and does change in an instant. What we think will be normal may turn out to be very far from it. However, my sweet hubby, Andy, and son, David, are chomping at the bit for a new family member soon. Maybe I will be writing about the adventures of a new fur baby in the future. I am hopeful. My goal for the future? My dream? To keep being a mom, wife, friend, and a mom to a fur baby again. To share my love, our family's love, and our passion for dogs, animals, and their well-being. We hope to bring a new puppy home soon, as she will be such a healing for our souls and hearts. My therapist came up with the idea of having this new puppy go through the K9 Good Citizen Program so she possibly could be a therapy dog for others too. This sounds like a beautiful thing. We hope to keep working toward making dogs, animals, and our worlds more compassionate and caring places. And we hope to spread the light and love once again in the name of all good things and in honor of dogs.

> Dear Anne, Andy and David,
>
> Our heartfelt sympathy goes out to you. As Labrador lovers (we've had 4) and animal lovers, we can't imagine such loss and all at once. Please know that the community is still praying for you and hoping you know that!! I will send a longer letter under separate cover but we wanted to do something in loving memory of your dear dogs and in lieu of the fact that we didn't make it in time to donate to their vet bills.
>
> Our Sincerest Condolences,

CHAPTER 8

Finding a Voice and Rights for Animals

Why did I choose to write about this you might ask? Writing has always been a form of therapy for me. I love writing. I used to have a sweet "chi" blog through Squarespace.com. It consisted of my love for our dogs and all good things in around the bay area where we live. I would love to see some of our laws change on the treatment, neglect, and abuse of animals. They are not our property. They get such little respect and have so few rights. In addition, I think many, many pet lovers would gladly pay for emergency transport if their beloved pets were ever in an accident and needed emergency medical care. **We need to create a more caring and compassionate world for all, humans and animals.** The news every day is more than brutal. It is *insane*. Animals bring therapy, peace, love, and care to us, without asking for much, if anything, in return. Think about all of the service dogs and the many roles they play. They should be more front and center, regarded with more esteem. If you're a lawmaker and reading this, please vouch for animal rights and help support them. New action and laws would be fantastic. There are many, many citizens who share this sentiment and would support you on your mission and brave endeavor. I am one right here.

In the meantime, we will keep on being grateful, praying, supporting each other through the tough times, and remembering our moments together with Sadie and Chuds. They will always be in our hearts. Never replaced, always remembered and revered for the great dogs that they were.

I believe in the healing power of music. There is an amazing song by Colin Hay called "Beautiful World." If you can, listen to it. It speaks tenfold on finding beauty in this chaotic world. Tonight I walked our loop alone, yet I could feel their spirit with me. As I tried to soothe my soul with Coldplay's "Hymn for the Weekend," I looked up to the stars and felt them there. They did not die in vain.

No matter what kind of pets you may have, they are an honor and a gift. They teach us so much about life, without saying a word. People often don't understand that. We can be so cruel to animals and each other. It's mind-boggling. We can be the most disgusting of beings and then some of the most incredible beings.

Another thought on incredible human beings. You know who you are. As one stranger wrote in one of our many condolence cards, keep on putting good into the world. Pay it forward. Share kindness. Do not let yourselves become bitter. We are blessed beyond words with the friends we have made throughout the years. You are very much our chosen family. Your everyday light, love, support, wisdom, kindness, humor, and genuine souls are what light our candle of faith inside. You make us better people and everybody around you. We may not have tons of money in the bank, but with friendships, families, and love, we honestly won the lottery. Thank you. You are so near and dear to our hearts and so loved.

Listen and tune in to your pets. Marvel in their simple wisdoms and unabashed love. They represent the better parts of us. Cherish the time with them each day, and savor in the moments. They are true gifts.

Dogs make us better people.

In memory of our dear Sadie and Chudley.

You were so brave. Always in our hearts.
May your doggy angel wings fly strong.
We will see you among the stars tonight, and every night,
until we meet again in a more peaceful place.

Thank you for everything.
Always, always with love.

AFTER LOG

Thank yous, Mahalos, Gratitude, Love, and Appreciation to Many Souls

One of my favorite things to do is give thanks. There are so many of you who deserve thanks. Many I have never met. Some are from my past, Andy's past, or our present. Here we go!

My husband, Andy, you are my rock, our son, David, our love and joy; Dr. B.; Dr. J.; Los Gatos Cat & Dog Hospital; Sage Animal Hospital; the strangers in the waiting room at Los Gatos Cat & Dog Hospital who generously and anonymously donated to our vet bill that morning; Bruce Wagman; Elisa; Outskirts Press; Starbucks Coffee; Peet's Coffee; Los Gatos Coffee Roasting; Philz; Nikki; the 'hood and community; the Haywards Heath Girls from days long ago; Homestead High peeps; Saratoga High peeps; Chico State; Cal Poly; San Luis Obispo; Dr. J-Law-Maq; iTunes; Spotify; J. R.; PrideZion Labs; Thornwood Labs; Beloved Labs; Mini Cakes by Tasha; The Posse; the Homestead High Girls; all of my dear friends; all of Andy's dear friends; Klara, Sandi, and Jaymi @ LGC & DH; Dr. S.; Pets 'n' More;

Petfood Express; Jillian @ Alaska Airlines; Don Miguel Ruiz and his book *The Four Agreements*; Petco; Chewy.com; Vet Source; our neighbors-you are the best; our community of Saratoga, Los Gatos, and Campbell; the teachers and staff at Rolling Hills and Marshall Lane Schools; Cupertino School teachers and friends; Aldo's in Santa Cruz on the Harbor; Deepak Chopra; Michael at Youth on Course at Poppy Hills; Cinnabar Golf; John at Linksoul; The Urban Pooch; my PTSD care providers; the police departments of West Valley, Los Gatos, Campbell, Palo Alto, Redwood City, Union City, and beyond; the paramedics; the fire fighters; the doctors and nurses; the vets and vet techs; my teachers; my students; my mom; my dad, who is up there with them among the stars; my family; my friends who are like family; the family we have never met that so kindly made a donation in honor of Sadie and Chudley to the Humane Society; the strangers we have never met who reached out to us and supported us during the storm; and all of the animal and dog lovers. Also to L. B. Johnson, author of *The Book of Barkley*. Your story has helped us tenfold in healing. You are a most talented and gifted writer. We share a passion for our Labs.

We are so blessed by *each* of you. Thank you. xo xo xo

PHOTO COLLECTION

Sadie and Chudley and Their Friends, including Dreyfus

Art by Paige Mason.

"What we have once enjoyed we can never lose.
All that we love deeply becomes a part of us."
-Helen Keller

Do you see the heart shape in Sadie's eye-her right, our left?

The watercolor painting is by Phoebe Chou and Ally Welke,
seventh grade students, neighbors, and friends in our community.
Their statements with this beauty were:

"Your life was a blessing,
your memory a treasure.
You are loved beyond words,
and missed beyond measure.

A special place within our hearts is always kept for you. xo"

Sadie, Chudley, and Dreyfus outside Starbucks Coffee.

Ever notice that dog spelled backward is *god*?
Perhaps He was onto something here.

A community of dog lovers.

Fri. 2/12/16 Saratoga News "

SPEAK OUT

LETTERS

Saratoga going to the dogs, and it's a lot of fun!

As a long term Saratoga resident, I had to share this candid photo from [Feb. 4] at our local Starbuck's (on Cox Avenue near Gene's Fine Foods).

One of the many things we love about Saratoga and Los Gatos is that there are plenty of dogs. Businesses in both towns seem to welcome our furry friends, leaving water dishes outside for our thirsty pooches, and such. (Not to mention we have some of the most stunning scenery to walk amongst, from the parks, trees, mountains, greenery, open space, the cute towns, etc.)

Today, all of us locals got together for a good walk and talk: seven dogs (Dreyfus, Bell, Cody, Murphy, Sadie and Chudley), four women (Saratogans Anne Palmer Peterson, Jen MacQuiddy, Helen Jarrett and Tacey Tucker)—one vet (three dogs), two teachers (two dogs) and one mom (one *big* white fluffy dog).

[We're] thankful for our coffee spots in Saratoga, friendly neighbors and furry friends.

ANNE PALMER PETERSON
Saratoga

PHOTOGRAPH COURTESY OF ANNE PALMER PETERSON

Anne Palmer Peterson, Jen MacQuiddy, Helen Jarrett and Tacey Tucker, all of Saratoga, are pictured with Dreyfus, Bell, Cody, Murphy, Sadie and Chudley.

We love our dog-friendly communities around us.

Art by Sabrina Hoeke.

Eyes are windows to the soul.

Chocolates love chocolate. Good boy, Chudley.

Evening stroll in the setting sun.

Love knows no boundaries.

Always in our hearts and our home.

May we meet again in dog heaven.

St. Francis of Assisi, saint of animals.

Perhaps they are not stars, but rather openings in Heaven where the love of our lost ones pours through and shines down upon us to let us know they are happy.

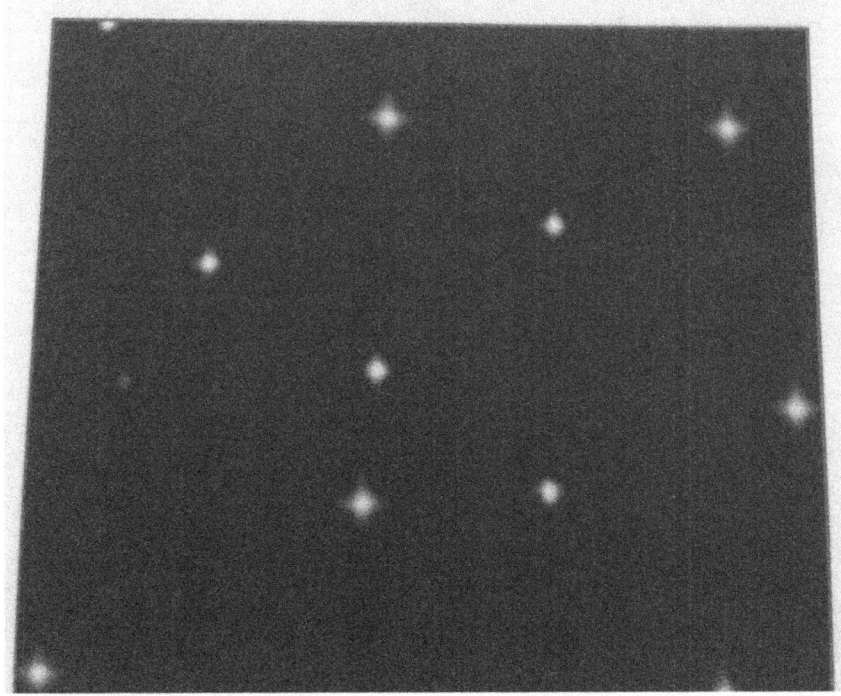

All lives matter. Go in peace. Let love rule.

www.ingramcontent.com/pod-product-compliance
Lightning Source LLC
Chambersburg PA
CBHW020022050426
42450CB00005B/597